Underworld

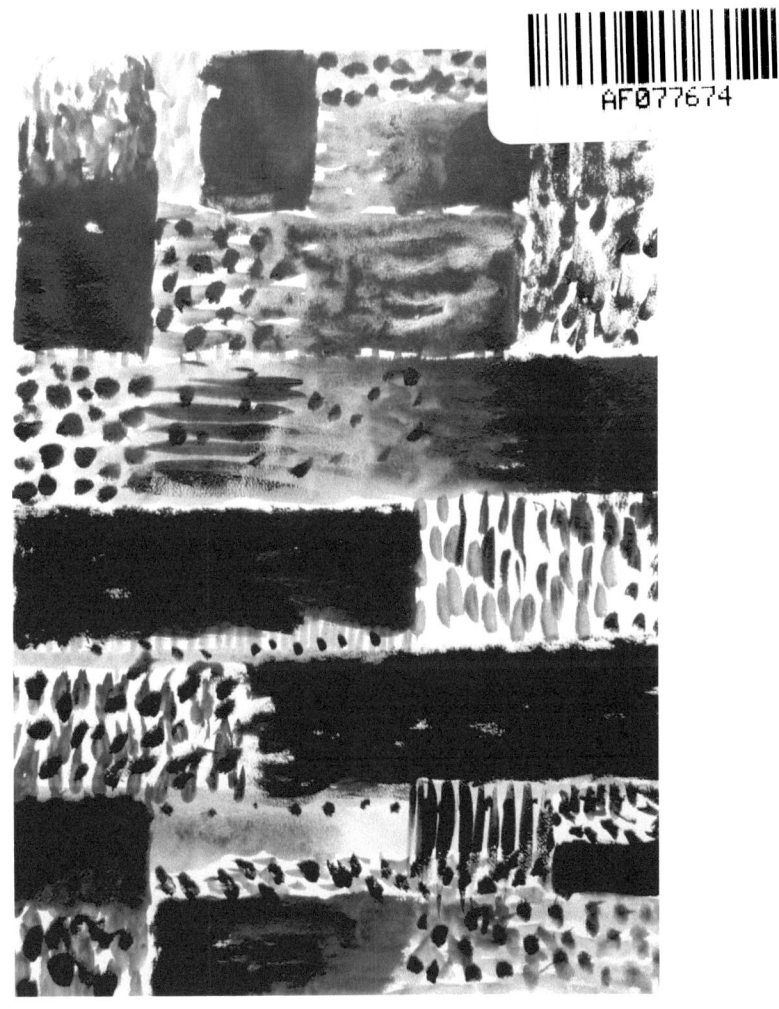

Words by Katherine Sutherland

Images by Alex Singleton

Underworld

Copyright © 2009, Katherine Sutherland and Alex Singleton

ISBN-13: 978-0-9556858-2-8

Published in 2009 by 'Web of Wyrd Press'
An imprint of BECS Ltd.
http://www.myspace.com/webofwyrdpress

All rights reserved. No part of this book may be reproduced or utilised in any form or by any means, electronic or mechanical, including photocopying, recording, or by any information storage and retrieval system, without permission in writing from the publisher.

Acknowledgements

Our thanks to Payam Nabarz for his assistance with this project; also to Jane Wyatt for proofreading the text.

Underworld

Lucid

They say I was taken, but I went willingly -

drawn down deep into the distant dark;

they say that I fought, but they mistook

my passion; ecstasy seeming fear in their eyes.

A choice was made, somewhere in cerebral depths,

a wet coal-black obscurity, high in a coffin of bone,

beneath the shiftless seams, to dream myself

immortalized; by want, if nothing else.

I chose to lie on the bed of the world,

in the birthing waters, newly opened to the night;

Sovereign, among the restless dead exalted,

exhumed as the light penetrated within.

Coughing the earth from my mouth,

pupils searing before the enemy sun

I returned, red lips, brazen hips, to tell my tale,

in the cold hard light of the blindness before dawn.

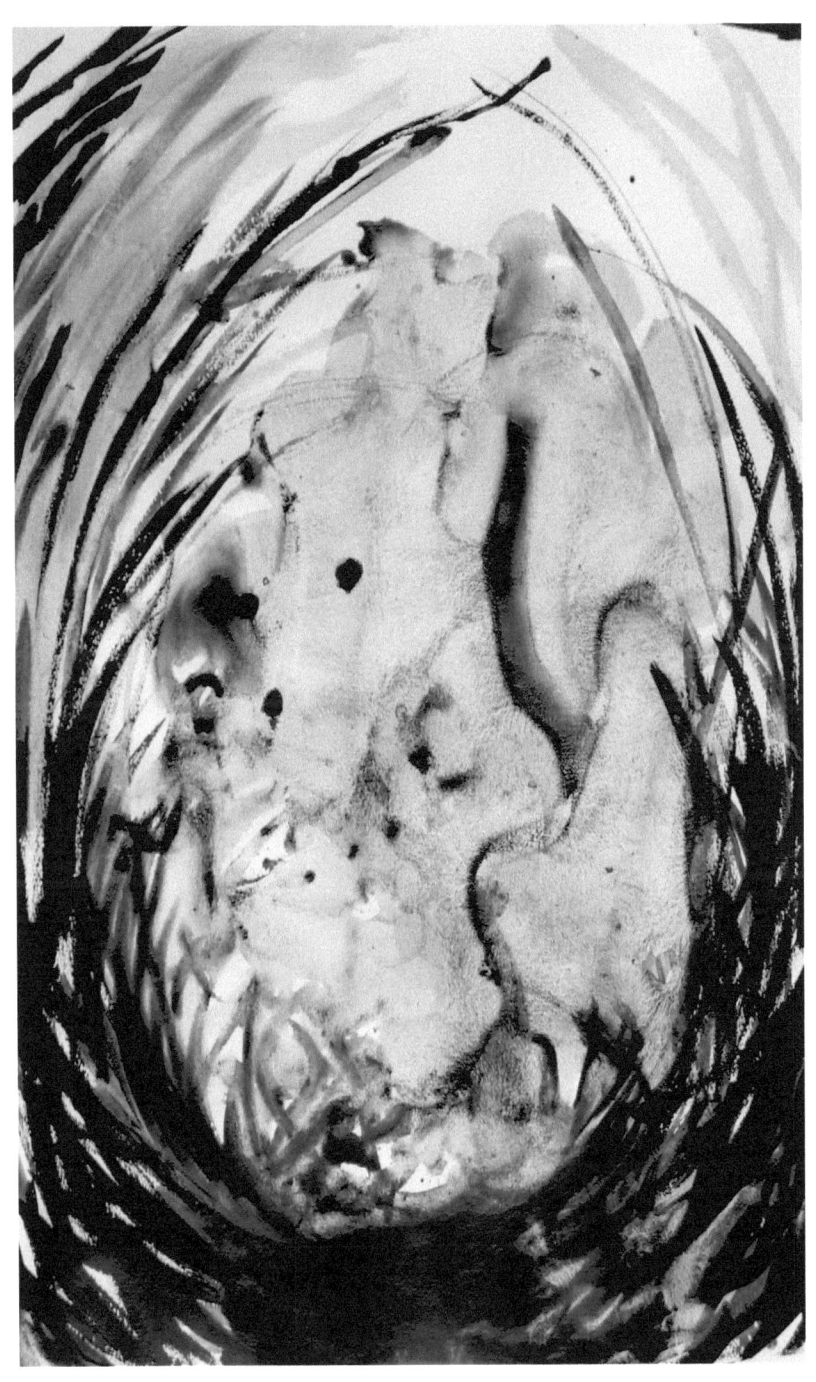

Beneath shiftless seams ...

Judgement

For centuries I walked the earth

a marble-footed pilgrim,

footprints as transparent as glass;

gazing skyward, at the heavens'

absolute ascent;

Dancing across the fields

as the night ripped open

the golden fabric of dusk,

and the figures of birds scaled

the heat, heavy with summer's sun.

One day, I knew, another would come

to bring judgement. How strange I was

to myself then, lost in the day dreams

of eternal light cast by the yellowing lamp of Helios,

across the pleated fields of overlapping homes.

I felt then, the ache, of the flower

that grew at my centre,

that could not bloom in this hot house,

this light-prison that would torch it to a cinder.

That power was speechless, unknown,

but for the fluttering in my chest

and the plague of tension, strung out

within me, colourless; the wrong pain.

So, discerning the ticking of time's hours;

I had to choose. To suffer sublimely in unending

summertime, to smile sweetly while my inner self

gnawed at the truth. I knew;

back then nobody even mentioned the C word!

Caught in my eye, the meadows,

flanks still warm from the sun,

breathing, intricate, a world

shaped from carpets of flowers

and a mineral tincture of dyes;

I looked around me, said silent goodbyes.

As night ripped open the sky ...

Above Ground

My life had been walled with the scent

of new-mown hay, of shorn wool, and

shadows that lengthened gracefully

with the slant shift of the light.

What we intend, what we allow to happen

is anyone's guess. I was tired

of earthly beauty, that's for sure;

consider my body, changeable,

incomplete, yet continuous.

It held the perfect likeness of former selves

that I was not, it casually renewed, formed,

budded out where I had scarcely noticed.

My purpose – to be transformed into

something that I could never find here,

so propose what you like – I saw causality;

the notion of the self and how one thing

follows another, in grim succession.

Every time I slept, I was deft in my dreams,

but they would evaporate before I could

grasp their details.

Something about me, footprints in the snow,

this dream self distinct from the person

I seemed in waking.

Light-footed, a holy unclouded soul,

I ran, tracking these footprints past the

snake-barked trees and beyond,

to the edge of darkness.

Then the details blur and melt away,

only a momentary afterlife of joy,

the body solid again, the mind a distraction

the net of the slipshod world,

entangling my tell-tale heart.

A momentary afterlife of joy ...

Descent

My mother slept, still I sat,

until my breath was going away,

driving me forestward, across the patchwork

meadows, to flash into the shadows.

All were at rest, but the sun,

and a dove, quiet on a treetop.

I think I moved through the left half

of my brain, which moved my right,

which danced my body onward,

Windblown; should I continue?

I paused at the edge of light and

considered, what was out there.

Not the shadow of a person,

or the echo of a voice, timbre

strangely different, after dark.

The answer was strangely concealed

within myself; there were fathoms between

Us, but we were familiars, I am sure of that.

Mystery is what apprentices seek

to be trained in, so I asked the question,

Who will teach me? The answer, expectedly

ironic was no louder that the sound of my own

blood forcing in my veins, beating a drum of life,

as I waited on the precipice to step over the edge.

At once, the night was ringing, with singing,

strange ethereal sounds of beauty that

could rip out your soul and spit it to the depths.

As I fell into the dark, I bid the light goodbye,

free falling headlong into the unknown.

The impact was shattering in every sense.

World, bone, and life. I became a faultline of myself,

spinning a cycle on the spindle of time.

I could hear *them* cackling at the base,

of the tree from which everything is rooted.

As I stood at this altar underground, I could feel it,

feel it coming, something of the unknown,

and I sensed the fear shining about my brow,

of the road before me, widening, my gaze

owned by my fixation on the purple black gloom.

I had no nerve endings to carry sound,

time enwrapped me on a needlepoint,

in the night, words wandered,

like shadows in my head

As I wound down, down,

like a spring uncoiling,

down in rock folds, smooth

as marble or polished obsidian,

towards the crystal cave, at the centre.

The world above had developed requirements

that I could neither articulate nor meet;

I knew I had grown to this out of want,

slowly, while everything sped onwards.

Step by step, I wound myself down,

down into the depths of the earth;

the lover, the father, waiting,

 in the ripening vegetable darkness.

Time enwrapped me on a needlepoint ...

Sub Terra

Some are afraid to be underground,

but not I. Some fear the pressing of the

blood-red walls, the birth pangs remembered,

deafening to the ears. My mother screamed

when I was born; nobody listened.

I always knew I was happier, before I was born.

Down in the phosphorescent depths,

doubt clouded my breath, but I forged on

the path of forgetting. My feet carried

me on their own rhythm, the dance of death,

beautiful, yet terrible to those who look upon it.

I don't remember arriving; only my nagging thirst,

that burned harsh and chemical in my throat.

I am only told that I sank down low on the waiting

soil and embraced it, my clothes were stinking

and clinging to my ringing body; which shone

hard as a sweet kernelled nut.

The river water had swum into me,

slow, black and inviting, cascading

velvety waves of the past, the present,

that yet to come and the no-time inbetween.

So I slept, and they tended me.

wrapped in a star shroud,

anointed with perfumes of the night, polished hard

as a coal black diamond of illumination.

Yet I knew I was waiting, watching him,

watching me, both of us contemplating

our next move in the dance.

My feet followed their own dance ...

Helios Gamos

Allow me to translate myself,

to blow through the branches of your bones.

I am blessed with two tongues, one above ground,

one buried deep within the keening depths.

Both my tongues wear red gowns,

drip blood in the sharp declining west,

and both cut me in half when we make love.

Is it they or I who got displaced?

They sing different songs in

half-dug trenches. One a spade

travelling south, the other reaching

north and skywards.

I hear them, knocking through the soil

to meet me, like two escapees, digging

in the same warm dark tunnel of time.

And I cannot know that these two diggers

loathe each other, have not spoken in years;

but I will be a conduit, for thought,

feeling, of anger and wit,

of two sides of the same debate.

I had climbed the depths,

to where the stones were calling,

and the flower within me

was opening and speaking;

they heard nothing,

nothing to hear, heard silence.

Still I climbed to where

that flower was chanting,

down the winding path

to the underworld,

where the Gods were waiting.

I cannot describe the beauty of his face.

It was painful to look upon,

the gentle deep power, brimming forth

through the pores of his blackened skin,

aged and ageless. I cannot describe the dignity

with which he reigned, sovereign supreme

without saying a word,

seed king, waiting in the dark,

potential bound within his being.

And he was so quiet.

Not a ranging annihilating God,

but a gentle lake eyed beast of love.

To me he was the alpha and the omega,

the eye of a needle through which I

threaded myself to stitch a bright pattern

of my own design, there,

to map the key to my existence.

Warp and against weft,

we wove together, not speaking,

yet knowing the truth was in our rapture,

my ecstasy the breath of a thousand years

of misconception, being gently worn

away by the tides,

the flowing of our time spent

shipwrecked in each other's arms.

And so we danced, red queen and white king,

perfect alchemy in his knowing smile,

seeding dreams in the dark places

that the sun does not know.

and I thought this time could last forever,

I did not dream there would be

a time when I would go...

Forbidden Fruit

Many get this wrong, but actually he

was the one with conscience;

he talked of my earthy duties,

said that my mother would miss me.

I thought my mother was quite grown up enough,

she could manage on her own, fine thank you,

as she had all too often told me.

And so my disbelieving ears swallowed

the notion, that I was to return to the light.

I cried when I heard this,

for in the darkness I was Queen,

a loathy sovereign of souls

caught betwixt the worlds in earthly death.

My heart tore in two

as I contemplated this parting,

I could not bear never to drown

myself in the great dark lakes of his eyes

again, never to die the petit mort

in the glimmering hall of his arms.

Contrary to popular report,

it was I who took the fruit;

a hard, dark pomegranate

that shone like a lamp

in the blackness.

I knew that he was sorry to see me go,

He even murmured something about,

"If you love something, let it go"

or some other common phrase

that the gods use to excuse

something they do not like,

a hasty decision,

formed behind the eyelids

in a nano breath.

It had been spoken.

 Language gives us our existence,

but there was so much more

that remained unsaid.

His eye, on its own trajectory

betrayed the honey

that lay sticky in his heart,

where as a bee I buzzed,

lazily drinking

myself beyond the pale.

I never thought

to see a god cry, his silence sliding

down the architecture

of his face,

dropping softly away.

Forbidden fruit ...

The Promise

I put a brave face on it;

a woman has to in these circumstances.

I was going, yes, but I was also returning,

as the sea loves the land,

as the moon loves the sun,

as the skylark the new dawn and

the nightingale the twilight;

my feet were sure they knew the path.

Of course I had been warned

never to eat of the otherworldly fruit,

'Look where that got Adam'

my mother warned, 'so keep your wits

about you my girl, even if it beckons

with desiring fecund flesh.'

As I took that orb and held it

within the folds of my skirts,

I knew.

If I let it touch my lips

I would be found for eternity,

handfast with the darkness,

and that what exactly what I wanted.

The fruit, innocently sang its song

of the night, shattering my inhibited

fears as I turned away from him,

 supposedly for the last time.

As the power flowed through me,

the fabric of my being was torn forever

into a garment of two halves.

I don't know if he felt it too,

that renting of seams and fibres,

forced apart to sit at opposite poles

of the spinning gyre of time.

Born into the light, yet seeded in the dark,

I became a circuit, flowing

out of the well head, yet drowning

in the beauty of its deep black waters.

And I knew I had made a promise,

a promise of my own choosing,

to return to my lover, to see

him rise and fall again

on waves of desire, as I,

a small vessel of the night

lay run aground

upon his brackish shores.

My feet know the path ...

In The Dark Country

The way out seemed much longer

than the way in, I don't know if it was

because I didn't really want to leave

him there in his kingdom, while I, his bride

in heaven journeyed far

away as a compass point.

I knew our hearts were as one,

but still I feared the distance.

Somehow I grew smaller,

my grandeur dwindling,

and I wondered if I was a fool

to even think that he,

the great Underworld God

could ever love me.

Then the seeds shouted to remind me,

that fate had brought us together in secrecy,

beyond my mother's tears.

It is odd that there were no arguments

before I left, the decision to make the journey

welled up from deep within.

When I returned I was sure

there would be plenty,

but I would not heed cross words,

for I had given away something

that could never return,

and in this death, I had become my whole self,

with the right to choose.

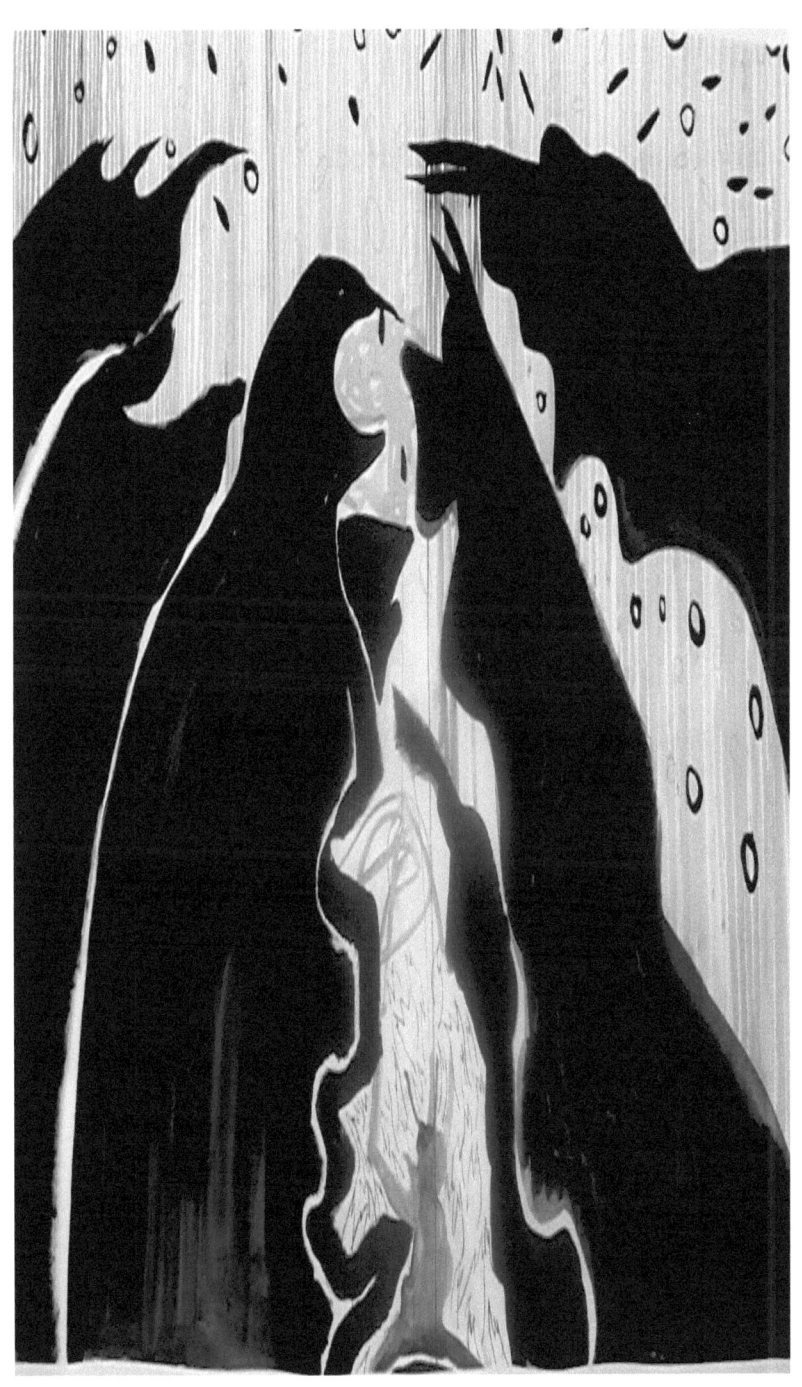

The great underground ...

Ascent

Footprints inside each other, I climbed

up stone steps towards the blue skies,

then it struck me that something was wrong

and I became frightened

about how long I'd been gone.

Nothing could be heard,

but the breath of a scream,

alluvial in the dark; no bird song,

no animals grazing, gone from my memory

were the scents of summertime,

the joyful field-dance

on golden wings of light.

Slowly, the realization dawned

in the black wet space, the casket of my head.

What had I done?

Shame formed, puce in my temples, spreading

like twilight from my hard dark heart,

shrouding me in a cloak of grief.

The land had receded from me,

and I from it, and with me all the happiness

that I garnered from my mother's breast.

What to say? I scarcely knew. My bones ached

with longing for my mother's heart,

DNA spiralled, snake-like in its reach for her,

but fear knocked a stronger rhythm

in the fibres of myself.

How to explain?

That I had been rent into pieces

by my own choosing, that I had revelled,

in the light of the darkness and sailed

the mystical ocean and

islands of dreams within his grasp.

It was too hard, too big a task;

all hope ebbed away,

until my voyeuristic gaze caught

a faint glimmer and trapped it,

prisoner in my eye until my brain

could decode it, could fathom

the shape into meaning.

Two torches sparked about the boundary place,

and that could only mean one thing.

She was near; sister to my mother,

older, more likely to understand

rather than dismiss the whims of my heart,

which I knew my mother would call foolish.

Guardian of the gate, key keeper,

her voice rose, out of the gathering gloom,

the question not framed as a question,

but an affirmation of what she already

knew; "I know where you've been,

your mother's heart is broken

into shards that pierce her every breath."

I bowed my head, not meeting

 her fire formed gaze, but I knew

as she spoke, that I would have to face her,

to be judged and found worthy.

It was not a sin that I had committed,

for I had married the darkness

in solemn pledge to be true

to every side of myself.

The winding path ...

Consolation

My mother's face framed my fear and love;

and all at once I was her little girl again,

apple of her eye, fruit of her heart,

but I carried a moonless secret

deep within the walls of my soul.

She was angry, that is true,

she raged and flew at me,

crushing me hard in an iron grip of

one who cannot believe their luck and must

hold tight to it, lest it disappear

like gossamer threads

 into the fine thin air.

She knew I was changed, yet told herself

I was not, in that sweet deluding way mothers

always keep their children in their bosom at

a certain age of tender innocence.

I had to explain that the choice was my own,

and however many trees she uprooted or

storms she cause to course the land,

my mind and heart had made their choice.

She wept then, when she knew my foundation

was unshakable, though she cursed those

who laugh about the tree for allowing 'us'

to come to some great togetherness

in the Underworld.

She questioned me as to whether I

had forgotten the fate of Psyche?

I said I would rather know once

and remember that love,

than forget forever and go back,

for a path walked in the wrong direction

never leads to a good ending.

So that was it.

She accepted my choice eventually,

with good grace.

I'm sure there will never be a gathering,

a tea party of the gods, but she agreed to tolerate,

which is good enough for me.

Illumination

I like to think that we all learnt something here,

by my earthly descent to the depths of my love.

I know now as I think I always did,

that the light cannot exist without the shadows,

for it is the light that causes the shadows to fall.

One can extinguish another,

a dusky breeze can end the life of a lamp,

in the same way that a candle

can chase shadows to the corners of the world.

But for how long?

One cannot be restrained by the other,

for if you rip out your heart by day,

overnight it will grow back.

Just as light creeps in

at a casement chink,

so shadows slink

underneath the door and creep

slowly up the walls.

Just as I could not remain ever pure

in the eyes of light,

a virgin bride wallowing

in meadows of unhappiness,

neither could I deny my heart

and the seeds that lay there.

So I am married.

 And in loving both, and embracing both,

I bring judgement and balance to the axis of my world.

About the author

Katherine Sutherland is a poet, teacher, storyteller and musician. Her interest in myths springs from listening to retellings at primary school, and the Persephone story has haunted her since childhood. After reading English at Oxford, Katherine lived in a variety of urban landscapes, yet this poem was inspired by the wildness of the Scottish Highlands that she calls her ancestral home. Katherine has written extensively on poetry and myth, completing an MA on the uses of mythical archetypes in modern poetry. Her poems have appeared in a variety of journals, such as *Touchstone*, *Fire* and *Magma;* and anthologies from *Forward Press*, *Avalonia* and in many other *Web of Wyrd* titles. She has also published a study guide on the poetry of Philip Larkin for sixth form and university students. Katherine works as teacher, inspiring her pupils with the dance of words, the magic of film and the power of stories.

About the artist

Alex Singleton trained at Central Saint Martin's College of Art and Design. After his degree he travelled extensively in Australia, where the intensity of colour and shapes of the landscape inspired him to develop a style and a language that he could call his own. In Australia Alex exhibited in a variety of venues including James Harvey Gallery, Sydney, and the Maclay Museum; he also completed a further degree at the University of Sydney. Alex now lives in Oxford and continues his artistic journey through generic portraiture and abstraction. He has recently hung pieces in the Royal Academy summer show, and participated in a group show at Modern Art Oxford. Alex works as a teacher, where he inspires pupils with the theories and practices of art on a daily basis.

www.ingramcontent.com/pod-product-compliance
Ingram Content Group UK Ltd.
Pitfield, Milton Keynes, MK11 3LW, UK
UKHW041433180426
11947UKWH00007B/419